Butterfly: Una Transformación

Author: La Espiritista

.

Illustrator: Nur Shojai

Life Chronicles Publishing
Give your life a voice!

To the Orishas who have been guiding, loving, and healing me my whole life through their wisdom and power. Thank you for reminding me that my queerness is embraced through my ancestral roots. Thank you for reminding me that I am a servant and messenger of spirit first and foremost always.

To my chosen family with whom my roots are interconnected underneath and deep within the soil of this earth. We shall rise with hands extended high into an illuminated sky. Thank you for reminding me that my strength can only be expressed more fully through our unity.

To all of my transcestors and ancestors throughout all planes with unconditional love source who have preserved sacred gifts for centuries, who have not abandoned me, this book has been birthed because of the seeds you planted a long long long time ago. Thank you for without you, I would not be.

May these prayers guide you towards your transformation now and always. Ase'.

Contents

Authors Note

Transformation- "Every person can become a butterfly."

The last few years, I have been retreating into myself much like the caterpillar retreats into their cocoon before it emerges as the butterfly.

I have been deep within an integration process of moving forward into myself entirely. This process has been grueling, to say the least. I am intentionally confronting and releasing past trauma. I have become aware that the cold-laden truth is that pain was never all mine to hold.

This pain has been carried for generations waiting for someone in the ancestral line to take responsibility for healing.

Someone who doesn't just put a Band-Aid on the surface and say, "It's all better now," but delves into the root of the wound to ensure the infection does not keep re-occurring.

I'm both lucky and unfortunate to be doing this work because it can be fucking hard.

It is extra challenging to do ancestral healing work when your connection to older generations in your blood kin is non-existent or strained because of your sexuality and gender due to that very real trauma you are trying to heal.

Throughout this process, I planted a seed.

The seed was for the manifestation of my first book of poetic prayer "Butterfly: Una Transformación," which has finally come to fruition. This book is ultimately about the process of transformation, which I have broken into four chapters: Release, Renewal, Retreat, Rebirth, to reflect the four phases of metamorphosis.

Metamorphosis is an act of faith.

This book is as much spiritual as it is queer.

I guess you can say it is a book on queer spirituality.

In the last few years, I have been reclaiming my spirituality.

When I came into my queerness, and then transness, I believed that there was no space for me in spirituality.

My upbringing is deeply embedded in Roman Catholicism on both parents side. Anything which slightly deviates the "norm" to their standard is inherently named a mortal sin, evil, or both, without much explanation.

While many of the teachings speak about judgment being only a supreme power of God....I can't help but see a lot of people judging.

I have come to learn that much of the teachings are interpreted through trauma and fear. That these teachings are used to control and exploit communities of color into submission.

Religious trauma is real.

I believe my purpose in this life is to heal and reclaim spirituality for queer/trans communities, especially those of color.

Both my queerness and faith are an integral part of who I am.

But let's get it straight (no pun intended), my spirituality is queer, and my queerness is spiritual.

They do not function as two separate entities which never relate; they are two entities which are always connecting and supporting each other. They are not two parts of my selves which never interact; they are always interacting because of my very existence.

I command to be seen as my full holistic being when I am in space. I am not only what you wish to see.

My sexuality is my spirituality.

Introduction to the Phases for Transformation:

Release: Release your grief. Release your old wounds. Release your trauma. Release your pain and heartbreak. Pray to the Gods, Spirits, Divine, Orishas who most resonate with you, to lead you to the door which guides you back to your original source. Ask for it to be unlocked, opened, and cleared. Start your journey back to the ocean of your origins. Allow her to hold, nourish, and nurture you.

Renewal: Joy is the resurrection of grief. Once you have allowed the grief to naturally flow through your body, explore the currents of your sensuality. Listen to the vibrant songs your being exudes as luxury. Watch the sunrise unfold into a prize of magnetic satisfaction. Touch the delicious curves of your own ecstasy. Taste the sweetness your honey is made from. Immerse yourself in your sexiness. Renew your pleasure. Renew your loving joy. Renew the voluptuous life pulsating through your veins. Paint yourself in gold and dance amongst a river of sunflowers.

Retreat: Through death comes rebirth. New life is within the dying of that which no longer serves you. Destruction from the most turbulent of storms brings forth innovative creation. Surrender into the darkness of your cocoon. You cannot exist without your darkness. Rather than allowing the darkness to consume you, allow it to integrate into the core of your being. Your darkness can empower your highest light.

Rebirth: Emerge in your radiant truth. Spread your wings and allow them to encompass the entirety of who you are without shame. Express your vision with unwavering confidence and exuberant command. You are the center of the dancefloor. You are the fire which draws people in. You are the charismatic flare which activates the cadence in their hearts.

You are the Pulse, Love

Release

1. Elegua

With my mouth full of sweet nectar;

Honey show me your rays. The ones which guide the wind and clouds

together to prevent a collision.

Crush obstacles the forest brings so

Osain may allow herb and spice to merge.

I will accept the sting rising above my throat,

So I may sing once again.

2. Solitude =/= Loneliness

Surrender.

Allow the bareness you contain to transform into space.

Fill it with the warmth you have been dying for.

Fill it with the warmth that you have been so wrongly deprived of.

Fill it with the warmth that you have so desperately needed.

Receive the richness from the peaks of radiance poured onto you at the beginning and end of each new-born day.

Reawaken to rejuvenation.

Her rays are meant to cradle you.

She is always willing to rock you back and forth, so you may drift into wondrous slumber.

Solitude does not have to equal loneliness.

It can be the light that complements the dark from the cloudiest of days.

3. Clouds

I do not remember the first time I overate, but I do know it was more than a decade ago.

I was probably sitting in front of the tv watching spy kids with my sister, Carmen.

We used to imagine we were the two kids from the movie, acting out every scene like we were following a manuscript, line by line.

I would always play the brother and the name of the sister just so happened to be Carmen.

A sweet coincidence that lured us into our future destinies, but the decision was always in our control.

4. Psalms

Even on the worst days you knew how to reset my breath.
You unclasped my hands, traced my palms,
and whispered through your fingertips,
"Growth does not have to be linear."

It can be a mountain range.
The highest hill top to the lowest valley.

5. Red Hands

My father used to sink so low on regular days.

The Christmas tree dismantled along with his spirit spilled his bloodline

onto the earth and raised demonic fire above the ground.

I wish he could have risen above the ashes,

but he shattered my dreams one after the other.

Gender and sexuality were taking a hold of me,

and my father caught me

arm and arm with a beautiful Korean girl

that I had gone on my first date with.

Infuriated he sent slurs of such hostility.

This is not a natural course he screamed on our drive home as the car

began to fog up from streams of hate. I could not help but wonder if his

rage was caused by seeing so much of myself in him.

6. Natural Course

Love is a cycle.

It is the beginning, middle, and end.

It is a full moon reigning in her most robust state.

It is half moon, a symbol of abundance not deficiency.

It is quarter moon the size of a fingernail guiding us in the direction of our personal journeys.

It is new moon restarting the phases again and again and again.

A realization that there is no need to worry over lack because we shall become full again.

7. Yemaya

The vision you bring to me is a crystal-clear horizon.

After all my thoughts swirl in turmoil,

you take my hand and guide me away from fear.

You cradle me in your ocean wide arms and

assure me there is no such thing as forever.

You remind me that to receive restoration,

there is a shoreline to be reached.

8. Focus

My mother use to tell me that the words "I want" were the words of
the devil.
That it was selfish and manipulative for me to ever hope or desire, a
world that I could co-create all on my own.
That it was better to focus on the outbreath of outsiders passing me on
the street, than to give recognition to the palm-lines on my own two
hands.
My mother has never learned how to openly listen to the way her breath
may waver when she chooses not to honor the sails of her own spirit.
She has never learned how soul loss occurs when she allows others to
steer her ship.
Even with this painful truth,
I want my mother to know my love for her runs deeper than my sea salt
tears.

9. Numb

Tomorrow I will wake up with ashes in my mouth

and cinder on the tips of my fingers.

Sirens will echo throughout my skull

and pound through the sockets of my lenses.

I am reminded to appreciate the simplicity of feeling anything at all.

10. 23

Therapy told me that my eating disorder was complicated.

That for me to recover I must discover

the deep-rooted issues inside of me.

That I must analyze and contemplate every

emotion, event, environment, element

about myself that ignited my urges to restrict or binge.

They said it would bring me closer to extinguishing its control and closer

to a full life.

11. Recovery

The first time I drank alcohol I was 14 years old. I downed a whole bottle of Georgie vodka because it eased my social anxiety. I have learned that I have never slowed down enough to develop a healthy relationship to being fully seen.

12. Uncoil

The process of becoming unchained is a commitment to be consistent
with our soul's calling.

It is intentionally responding to the nourishment our body craves without
guilt or shame. It is to bask in the immense glow residing in the most
guarded parts of ourselves, purposely releasing the trapped screams, so
they may transform to forgotten songs.

13. Free Life

Television told me that I wasn't supposed to be full.

That the girl I use to be needed to be empty.

At 16 years old I created a habit of self-destruction.

I was trying to mold my strong athletic 5'9 build to a petite 5'4 frame.

I wish I would have learned sooner that

my body is not meant for pretty pre-packaged boxes.

My body is meant for a free life.

A life that's full of time and energy.

14. Morning Dew

Lately I have been holding on by a thread.

Every breath is withering underneath my spine and

I am being buried alive.

I am salivating for the taste of new life, but my tongue continues to catch

leftover residue.

This cannot continue.

I am drowning, I am drowning, I am drowning

in an ocean full of sorrow.

15. The Exception

The forest is a watercolor painting floating in mid-air.

It gives you just enough room to hop on and enjoy a dreamlike ride.

The forest is the domain of dreams,

the doorway of enchantment and magic.

It is where fairies and human gather and don't always see each other.

They don't always see eye to eye, but you.

You can be an exception.

You see they rarely like your kind, but I kind of like you.

Let me be your guide.

16. Heavens Gift

Tears are cleansing.

They are fruitful.

Allow them to crush, cherish, and cradle you.

17. Extract

Squeeze me until I run dry like a lemon.

Let the sour taste in my mouth give a glimpse

of a bitter life left behind to embrace one of strong aroma.

Extracted from the purest coffee beans from the Valleres de Cuba.

Hold me until I am filled with juicy succulence

of coconut water from a place of origin.

18. Rain Callers

I am longing to live the way our earth celebrates every outpour.

She slowly absorbs the holy water into her skin,

until her complexion returns to a richness of dark brown.

This is a medicine to dip our feet in

which teaches us there is a higher purpose for why trees keep rooted and

raise their arms towards the sky.

My hands which once clasped so tightly together are expanding to make

room for the stars.

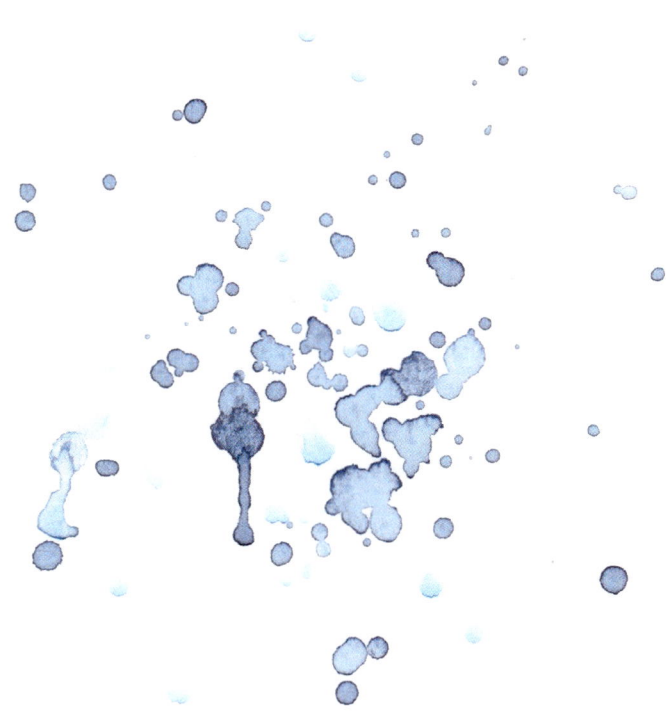

19. Unfold

Time can be found among the trees, whispering slow lullabies between each swaying leaf that has yet to let go of tempting wooden fingertips. Time can also be found coursing through jagged waves, rushing headfirst into unknown territory exploring messy and fragile ground, but finally coming clean.

20. Art of Allowing

Allow me to receive like the shoreline receives the ocean tide,

absorbs her cleansing foam,

and dampens each individual grain of sand with a mother's love.

Allow me to accept like ocean accepts the open vastness of her body.

Nourishes the ripples of her skin with kisses from the sun,

always welcoming what she deserves.

21. Your Lullaby

Love is the willow tree.

It is the rain she calls forth to bring cleansing to all living beings.

It is the protection and nurturing wisdom she holds at the core of her foundation.

It is the roots she digs deep into mother earth to create a solid grounding.

It is the ancestral knowledge she provides to make sure we begin to do our own work to bring our body, mind, soul, and spirit aligned.

It is the exploration of our full truths in all their colors; it is the messy and limited parts if ourselves.

It is the vibrant and expandable parts; it is the autumn leaves that transform and accept the lesson of free range.

It is the prosperous green that spring trees beckon flower petals to dance to.

A renewal from cold to warmth, a renewal of restful lullaby to a song that speeds your heartrate.

22. Release

The secret is in the transmutation of fear to faith.

23. Indigo Child

Crying is the ultimate release of the soul.

When I was young I remember being a princess and crying for the silliest things like not getting McDonald's for dinner.

I also remember crying for things that weren't as silly.

Like the time my father was teasing me about my hypersensitivity.

It was very subtle, but it meant so much to me.

I began balling and he told me to "Shhh. You are just like your Bipolar mother."

I learned to keep that silence deep in my bones for the last 23 years.

It is both strange and beautiful how the universe is so expandable, flowing, and ever persistent yet it is always pressured to be silenced.

If I have learned anything in life, it is that the universe's breath is time.

They breathe in and out and repeat the cycle again and again.

This is both a blessing and curse,

but I am choosing to focus on the blessings.

I used to constrict my chest with every out breath, but I am learning that my posture is much stronger when I choose to let go and give some love back.

I used to congest my lungs with every inhale, but I am learning that my interior can heal more fully when I choose to allow and receive that love right back.

I used to be ashamed of what lay in the core of my foundation,

but I am learning to honor and embrace the soil from which my seeds

birth new life again and again.

There is no wisdom in hiding your gifts.

I am learning I am learning I am learning.

I am sorry I am sorry I am sorry.

And I am forgiving, forgiving, forgiving.

I forgive you.

You,

The you that was me yesterday crawling through the debris of withered

flowers.

The you that will become the stems that catch fresh morning dew.

A symbol of release, renewal, retreat, rebirth.

Renewal

1. Oshun

You have allowed your tides to harmonize along to the vibrations of my voice.

Gently cradling each newborn word that dares to leave my lips.

We have met before.

Your waters have cleansed me, have graced me with new life.

They have carried away my old leaves,

And have kept the new ones to adorn the currents of your body.

2. Por El Dia

Hoy es un poema.

Por la manana la parte quando toda la vida, se ven con los ojos abrietos.

Ohos del color del cielo.

Mira, yo no se quando aprender hablar Espanol, pero yo creo el dia era un recuerdo abrazado por los angeles.

Angeles volando en un momento de cantar, una cancion mas grande que el mundo.

3. Fresh Eyes

Moments like this assure me that I am right where I need to be.

4. Ignite

Cradle me in your patient loving arms with each pebble rock step because sometimes the freedom of fireflies ignites a fury within I cannot contain.

Remind me that this path called my own winds and wobbles.

That it may be brittle and battered, but never broken.

Never hopeless.

There are streams along the way meant to replenish and renew until the next journey is in view.

5. Flow

I am smiling past the shame

that comes each time

someone tells me

I should be adjusting my pace.

I would be a fool not to honor my natural rhythm.

6. Joy

The sunrise is the imagination of spirit coming to life like our hands and feet. Dare to look close enough at them and I promise you will be able to see the tracing lines. Follow them to the moon. A crescent so bright that it reflects the beauty instilled in you onto the entire universe. Connecting constellation to palm lines and empty coffee cups. Drink deep from the darkness and richness within. Do not worry it will not consume you for it is the well of plenty.

7. Stranger

We will meet again.

Like the riverbed that eventually meets its point of rest.

Calm and serene,

Washing butterfly kisses and firefly sparks along our bodies.

All will be forgiven.

8. Turquoise

In between the rifts and ripples of blue

I can see the hopes of green in you.

With you.

Wrapped around my neck or hidden beneath the crevices of my body

pulsating my bloodlines with vitality.

My bones remember the first time they met you.

A familiar, but forgotten, terrain of rock and riverbed.

9. Quechua

My body is an earthquake of potatoes and cocoa leaves.

My bones a shrine of hollow rocks and legendary trees.

I am the fertile soil of the Andes.

10. Renewal

Sacred is the hymn that reverberates from rock to water. The joyful dance that dawns once one has taken the leap and allows their whole body clean. Tasting foamy lips and inviting cooling hands to wash away the deepest of wounds.

Inviting the sting to linger and the smell of red cedar to be drawn out. It is a stream of gold that is formed at the intersection of forceful ruins, the echo after the final fall.

11. Bee-Live

Surrender

is the sweetest of all stings

that never seems

to go away.

12. Limits

In my first reiki session,

I was told that my heart gave a unique experience to the practitioner working on me.

That his hand continued to expand, and he did not know where my heart ended.

He tried his best to contain my heart.

That is when I learned the difference between love and energy.

That my love is limitless, but my energy is not.

13. Heart Chakra

I want a love that is so expendable
my hand cannot tell the limits of
where it is confined. I want a love
that creates a connection so deep
there is no choice, but to delve into
the depths of another's ocean

14. Abundance

Beauty is the benevolent glow I share,
the ripened fruit gathered after a rich harvest,
tasting sweeter between the company of two.
I am learning to feel bitter stings between my lips,
while I speak my truth.
I am no longer afraid to catch the sun's rays.

15. American Gold

Joy is the resurrection of grief.

16. Whispers

Yo resido entre el reflujo y el flujo.

Mediar el ascenso y la caida.

Soy el susurro en el silencio.

Soy el movimiento dentro de la quietud.

17. Everlasting Love

All lasting relationships are grounded in the roots of friendship.

Anything else that may stem rises from the soil and flexes each cherry

blossom petal to the heavens.

18. Spider Senses

There is magic in the air when folx of color get together to share their
healing and care with each other.

There is love when one freely gives the truth they see beyond the
blooming stage to the full-blown web.

19. Heart Revived

Never have I tasted fresh fruit from the vine,
a harmonious invitation to pinpoint every individual beat pulsating up a
prickly line.
I can feel life as the warmth drains out of bitter body and the blood turns
a cool blue onto the palm of my hand.
This moment is the meaning of true warmth, a light I had not seen until
deciding to break open the darkest yet softest layer of you.

20. Sensuality

I am simmering glow; a frivolous essence slowly rising towards an
entrancing outpour.
I am ecstasy; an outburst of energy communicated through the vibrations
of orgasmic breath.
I am a volcano; an eruption so sudden.
One you never even saw coming.

21. Discovery Park

Es en el canto de la brisa fresca
y los gritos de la roca brillante,
que descubro mi lengua una vez mas.

22. Fluid

My sexuality is my spirituality.

23. Integration

Love is the riverbed.

It is the ebb and flow we must allow ourselves to lay in.

The deepness we must jump headfirst into,

the darkness we must explore

to emerge with our own true refuge of richness.

It is the jagged rocks along the way we must

overcome, breakthrough, return anew.

It is the healing of past wounds.

The willingness to engage the pain for beauty to emerge.

A remembrance that life is a lesson about integration.

That we must integrate our shadow parts to achieve equilibrium again.

Retreat

1. Oya

I pray for my death to be a gentle kiss.

For it to be a soft-spoken melody lifting my soul home.

For it to be the grace of fluorescent wings tearing free,

ascending to the light.

I pray for it to be the moment my heart stops from infinite love.

2. Soul Mates

The day the elder passed away was the saddest farewell.

I saluted in his honor and shrunk my head in defeat. I swore to find a

way to make peace with the lost souls who had abandoned ship amidst

their grief.

They had jumped off the plank submerging themselves in murky water,

sinking into the ruins of Atlantis.

I remember it as if it were yesterday, sitting by your side.

We shall meet again in this life.

Our hearts will integrate into the strongest most gentle ripple effect the

ocean has ever seen.

Together we will make the city rise again.

3. Wild

Death is the ultimate confrontation with the unknown.

It is majestic swan resurrecting from the journey of great mystery.

Death is the subtle ripples along her back.

It is the cleansing of reclaiming secrets lost at sea.

4. Starry Night

You taught me that silence is the key to rebirth, but it can also be the
chain that gags you to
death.

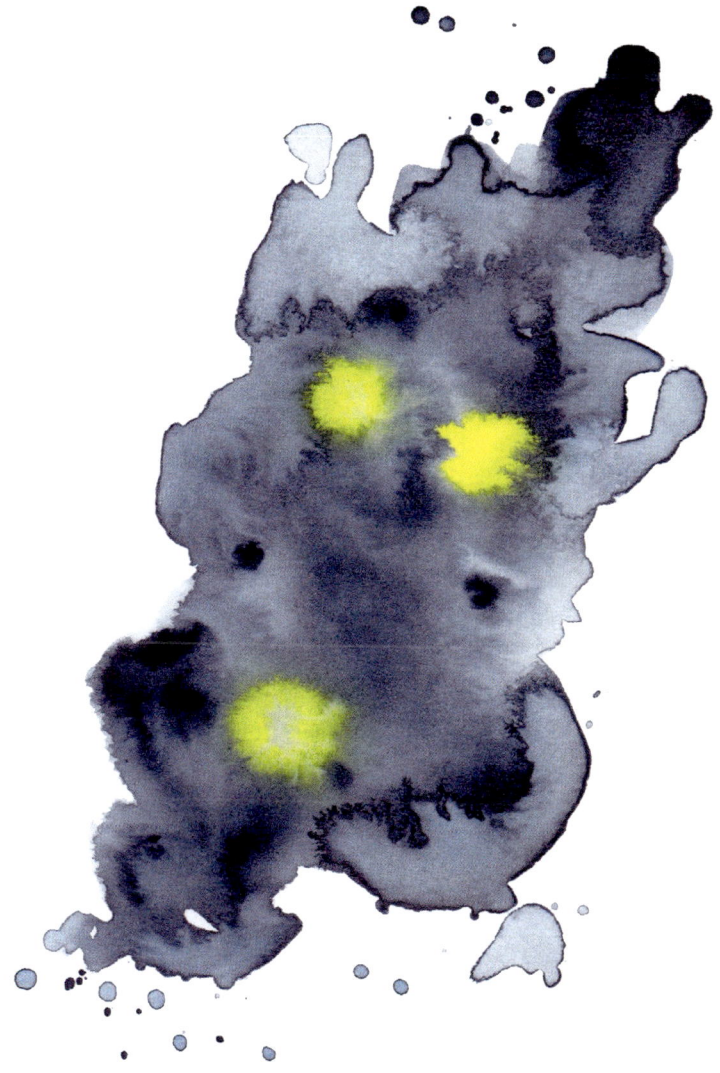

5. Dia De Los Muertos

El 1 de Noviembre, no pude ignorar sus susurros por mas tiempo.

Ascender, ascender, ascender,

regocijarse y deleitarse con la radiante reverencia.

6. The Fool

Take the Leap.

Allow the wind to guide your fall

and in the process remember your roots.

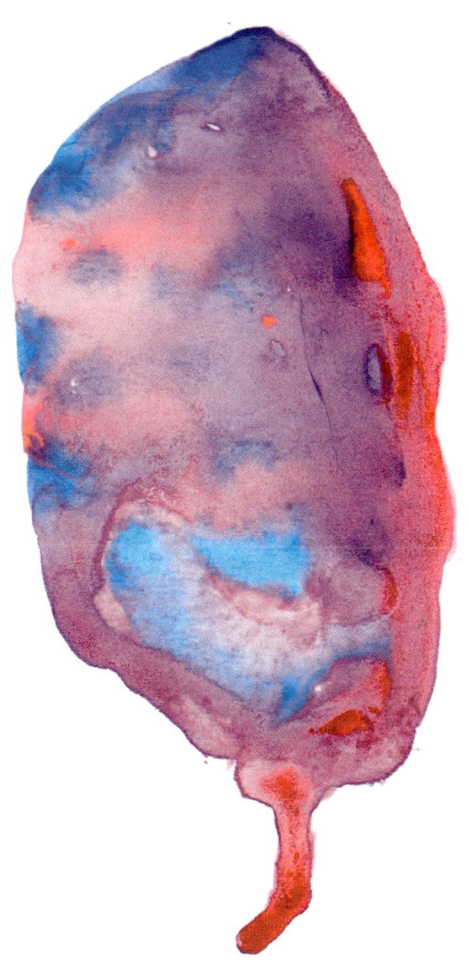

7. The Star

My ancestors are sending me scorching messages about letting go.

Heart wrenching sensations;

Smokey revelations strengthening my solar plexus,

finally freeing my light.

My throat loosens instead of stiffens and I sing to you

for solace, refuge, and guidance.

I pray to be divinely led into harnessing my power within these winds of

change that have gently pushed me West.

I am enthralled by dandelions breath,

sprouting from the seeds dispersed from a star's wish long ago.

8. Harbor

Sometimes I wish I could invent a story
with my own two hands the way you did.
To create a deep sea of transcending blue,
calm, yet violent in the torrents of a storm,
mustering its way to land.

9. Courage

The tides move straight towards the shore.
They flow underneath frost and bites,
refusing to be constricted to a frozen death.
The bareness left before unconditioned blooms
is an invitation to let things come to you.

10. I Forgive You

I'm sorry isn't enough they say.

For all the red extracted from your veins,

for the blue shipwreck your heart has become,

for the tender green aura your hands have lost touch with.

It isn't enough they say

but I listen to the color behind the voice.

11. Shadow

We are one with the ground and the sky, with fire and water, ash and air.

We are a generation meant to surpass all these elements, though our feet
can't leave the confines of sunken soil.

We have dirt underneath our fingernails from digging further into a hole
large enough to swallow us.

We are a generation lost, not erased, enveloped by the shadows we
create.

12. Serenity Prayer

Divinity and Devotion,

Gentleness and Grace,

Beauty and Bravery,

Indigo child, trust in the purity of your wings.

13. Transmutation

Sometimes the best gift you can receive is wrapped in the comfort of
your own skin, interwoven with the larvae being created to smooth your
transition from any foreign outbreaks. It is making the decision that hurts
the most but will provide the refuge for your greatest retreat.
This is worth the risk.

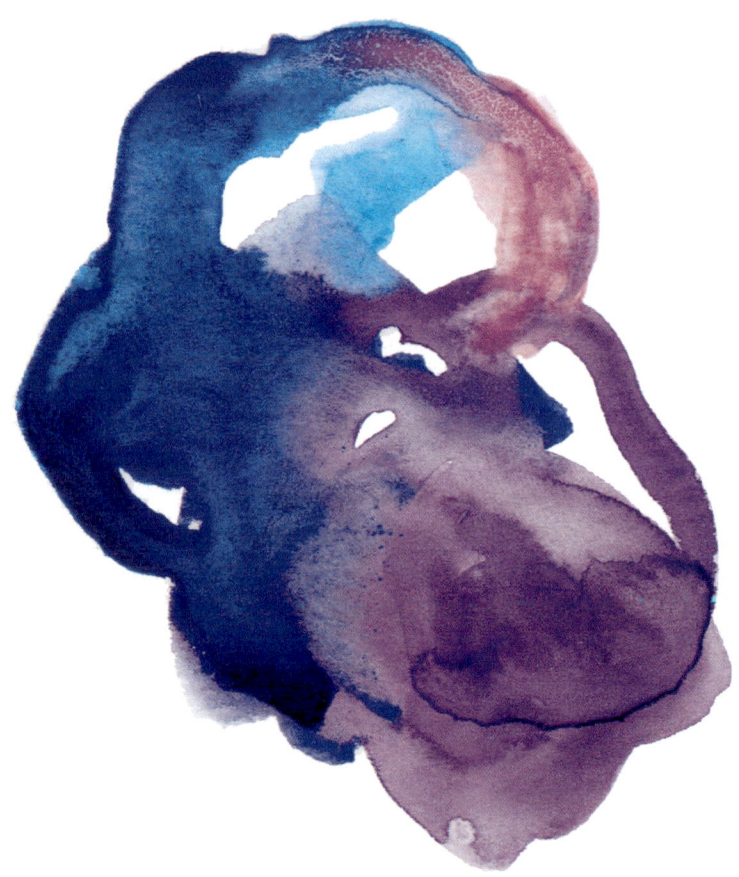

14. Beautiful Breakdown

I know it may seem hard to grasp, but I choose to sit with the pain.

I imagine my bones being broken down like a worn-down dining table.

I am first thrown over on my side where each of my legs are crushed one
by one.

My arms are folded and tied restricting the flow on my wrists.

The shattering glass of my heart is the loudest, exploding like a cork
from fine wine.

Waves of deep red embellish the carpet.

My sophisticated guests lose their appetites and rush away.

This is okay,

I am discovering true nourishment was never in their company.

15. Veil

I am frosty bite holding on by the skin of my teeth.

Chattering away; clashing at what needs to be un-frozen.

I am clammy in need of fire spoken touch,

to unchain me from this unspoken cellar room.

I am the Queen of Winter,

a beauty that freezes,

a goddess that has learned to let go and stand in her power;

the melting line between ownership and truth.

16. The Village

An intricate medicine of understanding death,

balances out an insatiable longing for life.

17. Opportunity

The sensation vibrating from the base of your spine to the crown on your
head is wisdom.

Listen to it in faith that it will provide just like the pyramids in ancient
times birthed kingdom from brick and stone.

Pharaoh commanded them into timeless structure, wished to surround
the world in gold.

Open your palms, choose whichever tools you desire.

Can you feel the world transpire?

18. Retreat

Courage is an internal flow of faith.

19. I Am

I am I am I am.

It is days like these when I'm wilting from exhausting fumes that I must
remind myself,
I have been waiting to blossom since birth.
I have been waiting to become fresh scent beauty,
a delicate gesture to one's hard gaze.
I have been waiting to be a sprouting masterpiece,
unique and special among its kind.
I am worthy of life because of my existence,
not for what I produce.
I am worthy for my ability to see
beneath the surface from which others overlook.
I am worthy for providing gentle grounding space,
even when one picks off my petals.
Worthy of life because I am.

20. Layers

Letting go is the slowest natural death

21. Storm

There comes a day when one must break out of the cocoon. A sincere sign to release the self-absorption, to set the wound to heal, to swim towards the hum of uncertainty where one can truly begin.

22. Sister Protector

Mi hermana mayor, I forgive you.

You were just a child too. It was not your responsibility to keep the
planets aligned and the universe in balance.

23. Faith

Love is the ocean.

It is the tides rushing to shore for safety in 49 individual grains of sand.

It is the individual who dares to ride each tidal wave.

It is the openness and width the ocean signifies.

A space big enough for all her children to challenge, learn, and grow
from each other.

It is a nourishing blanket meant to revive the breath of every being who
has sunk,

but then has risen between the waves a reclamation of power,

the faith that she will carry us home again.

Rebirth

1. Chango

I spill blood onto the sky each time your belly rumbles and strikes a

cadence I must dance to.

You and I are on the center of the dance floor.

We are the irresistible fire who attract people in.

Each step I take is an offering for you.

2. Balance

There is no need to rush.

3. Empowerment

My voice was constructed to build a foundation of truth.
My words are
meant to reverberate through hollow blockage,
dismantle outdated towers,
create a new path.

4. Amor es Amor

Love is balance. Amor es paciencia. Love is kind. Amor es amiable.
Love is vulnerability. Amor es humano. Love is feeling through the pain.
Amor es aparecer. Love is layers. Amor es entero. Love is being. Amor
es destruccion, Amor es creacion. Amor es presente presente presente.
Estamos presente. Amor es una invitacion. Love is receptive, love is
tamed, love is wild love is liberating love is free love is joy love is grief
love is essence. Love is spirit. It is life. Love is repetition. Always beating
again and again. Love is our natural rhythm thumping loud and proud
against our chests. Love is the universal heartbeat that unites us all; the
calling that beckons to create una nueva familia., Una communidad en
unidad. Love is our PULSE.

5. Rooted Wealth

To have a light

that lives deep below

the framework of ones bones,

a light which shifts the ground beneath ones feet,

when standing still.

6. Pride

Moments cannot be constrained. They are meant to be raised high by the intricate vibrations that reside in our innermost core. They are meant to fly fierce and bold like a blue jay in the light sky, so the entire world may gaze at their exuberant confidence.

7. Torch

I wish for the world to become a phoenix and ignite in flames.

To let the old ashes go astray

and embrace each newborn moment in love.

Love now because a goldfinches song can only be created

by one's own joy.

Love now because meaning is manifested

by one's own turtle shell.

Reach far into scorching ember to savor reborn feathers on your tongue.

8. Paciencia

We all have a radiant source within us. This fire rises, dances to the flickers of his own flames, and resets when the smoke gets too thick.

He scorches our bellies with marks of perfect timing.

9. Yemanya

Balance is a mother's love
washing over long forgotten wounds.
Balance is the stirring of a heart defrosting,
the warmth of a stranger's hand.

10. Leo Rising

I am no longer afraid of the fire within me.

It is the same fire which rises each time I watch my mother's tides fall.

It is the fire which cleanses her sea salt tears.

The same fire which rides the jagged waves within her veins.

My fire comes from the source of my creation.

11. Butterfly

Have you ever seen a cocoon after it cracks?

It's emerging brilliance with brightly-colored wings

free from confinement.

A history carved along old skin left behind for true fulfillment.

Fluttering wings like fluttering hearts.

Enriched with the enlightenment of blue skies.

12. Afternoon Tea

Pick me up, get to know me.

Sip slow,

let the intensity build in between two hands shaking

from the buildup of heat.

Allow the steam to fester, it will soon dissipate.

Put me down, don't look away.

13. My Lady

She was jaw drop, starstruck, misty eye material.

Her hair was a warm golden-brown aura,

a sweet essence swirl of ground and fire.

She was extending her arms to obtain the sun's rays,

absorbing and bathing in the kindling of his

ecstasy.

14. Sexuality

My favorite pastime is making love to colors.

Infusing essence and elements,

combining water and earth,

transforming air to fire,

creating consensual circles

around your back.

15. Genderfuck

Fluid and fuck are my favorite words.

Fuck for fuck your binary ideology.

Fluid as in I will be the ebb which trickles right through your constraints.

I am over, over explaining myself, so here it is plain and simple:

My soul is a fluid femme genderfuck.

Te rezo a ti todos los dias.

My spirit is free flowing with the harmonious range of the Andes

mountains and the tumbao of Havana's waters.

16. Soy Encontrado

Y por fin he encontrado a mi mismo en el poder de mi propia voz, la armonia del espiritu universal.

17. Oxumare

Surrender to the grace of rhythm the universe provides. Allow yourself to express through vibrations, slipping from sexuality into spirituality. To merge a bridge and be at one with all streams of consciousness.

18. Queer

I love my queerness.

It is a magical perk that peaks between the valleys of my smile.

It is the light-hearted approach, traveling through the cracks in my veins.

It is the lifeline I choose to invest in,

the treasure at the end of the rainbow.

19. QTPOC

I am a Queer Trans Person of Color,

but more specifically I am mestizo.

I am fluid.

I am open to many forms of intimacies and love.

I am choosing to be seen.

All of me.

I acknowledge and honor everyone

who is unable to choose and are living in constant fear.

I pray for the folx who have lost their lives this year and every year,

just by living in their truth.

Just by being.

I am choosing to celebrate QTPOC

Life for

All of us.

20. Metamorphosis

I love the colors that exude from my aura

when I'm entangled in my happiness.

It comes from the same solitary place I once longed to be freed.

An abrupt transformation from dark to light,

a super emergence of brand-new form.

My most natural metamorphosis.

21. Divinity

My collar bones are divine. I love how prominent and unapologetic they stick out, when standing tall and proud amongst a crowd. I love the unwavering certainty they convey each time I have the courage to expose them. They are defined through confidence, a foundation built by belief and faith. The trust that my voice is strong enough to carry the powerful being which has blossomed out of my

bones.

22. Cafe Con Leche

I am the dark magic, awakening the world's senses,

a guide for when dawn breaks between the clouds.

Yo soy La Espiritista

Espiritista, llamame para guiarte

Llamame para ayudarte

Llamame para restaurar.

I am the white light, soothing sound waves aiding humanity to slumber,

a guide for when night weaves through the stars.

Yo soy La Espiritista

Espiritista, llamame para guiarte

Llamame para ayudarte

Llamame para restaurar

Llamame

La Espiritista

23. Eshu

Great trickster I salute you,

Great trickster I salute you, Great trickster I salute you,

upon every new awakening.

My eyes unlock as you slip your keys in between angels and shadows.

You carry my dreams to sights unseen.

You are within the pulse of crashing waves, the tip of rupturing

volcanoes, the edge of high tide winds.

Acknowledgements

To my mother, for without you creating me, I would not be. Although the tides we have sailed have been rough, I still love you. You have taught me that through faith, nothing is impossible. Thank you.

To my spiritual family, the Orishas, angels, fairies and earth elementals, without your guidance I would not be the messenger I am today. Thank you for entrusting me with such noble responsibilities in this physical plane.

To my ancestors, without you I would not be. Your sacrifices have led me to where I am today. For that I am grateful. Thank you.

To my Abuelita Flora, you are the preserved image of the matriarch. You create an ocean of space for others and command what you need into existence. Thank you for sharing your power with me. It is okay to be afraid, but remember we are with you as you make this journey to the next realm. I am always holding your hand, but it is okay to let go. Con mucho mucho amor.

To my partner Noah, thank you for existing and loving me unconditionally. You are a reminder that there is life after death, and that both exist simultaneously. Your presence has supported me to follow-through. I love you.

To my illustrator Nur, thank you for providing the visual imagery to this creation. Your artistic talent compliments my way with words. Our spiritual connection has been invaluable during my metamorphosis. This book is a symbol of our collective transformation.

To my Baba, James Weeks. Thank you for believing in me, this book, and your spiritual wisdom, teachings, and guidance.

To my father, thank you for teaching me the lesson of forgiveness. Although our generational wounds run deep, you have taught me it is never too late to heal. I pray you find peace in this life and beyond. To my family members, Thank you for the message of never giving up and uplifting others-Roxy, Diane, Barbara, Colin, Sophia, Conner, and Chole.

To my sister, Carmen, thank you for supporting me through my darkest times, your forgiveness and love, and accepting the person I have been transforming into. You remind me to be unafraid of giving my love rather than hoarding it. Love is meant to be shared.

To my two-spirit and QTPOC family, especially everyone at Cura Club, but definitely not exclusively, thank you for reminding me we are always connected and that we are a community in unity. You all are a direct reflection of myself and a reminder that I am never alone. You walk with me wherever I go. Julz for your fierce libra ways and passion for healing. Ale for your loving laughter and deep-rooted wisdom. D.J. for your commitment to the movement and your tender heart. Karissa for your immense ability to hold space and share loving medicine. Giselle for your cosmic and galactic wisdom. Alex for being devoted to healing work and creating lasting connection, Stacy for looking out for everyone and always being down to call the four directions, Mere for your tender loving soul Amira for your vision of justice and true inclusion. Cesar for your solidarity and warm embraces., Rafaela/o for cultivating new ways of intimacy and sharing, Nic, Kim, Deja, Lee, Tate- thank you for your love.

To my mentors from Rutgers University, Zaneta Rago, Sharice Richardson, Liz Amaya Fernandez, each of you showed me to the door which was long obstructed from my view. Thank you for clearing the path for me.

To mentors and family at Seattle University Bernie, Tyrone, Bianca, Drea, Jalen, Matt. The rest of the SDA community. Each of you have gifted me in special ways. Thank you.

To my first chosen family, Thank you for holding me at such a turbulent and stormy time in my life. You all contributed to my survival. Justin and your family. Xavier and your family. Manny. Taleda. Jen. To dear friends J Mase III, Dylan, Jill, Tara, Will, Liz, Joie. Thank you for gifting me each in your own unique way. To my friends Angela, Batul, Melissa, thank you for sharing your knowledge of the plants and ancestors.

To past lovers who have taught me where I need to take accountability as well as show me what I will not stand for. For all the lessons we have gone through together, whether messy and/or smooth, I would not be who I am without you. Christie. Sam. Dane. Maileny.

To Vanessa, thank you for telling me about the butterfly. For the ocean of nurturance, nourishment, and love you gave me. This book would have not been birthed without you.

To the river, the oak tree, the stars, the infinite sky, and all the elements of this vast universe, thank you.

To all those who have touched my life with your light, who have inspired me to live as my most authentic self, who have been needing to witness queer spirituality, and who need to heal, be in faith, love, cry, and embrace complexity with simplicity at the same time; I salute you and thank you from the depths of my soul and spirit. Thank you. May you be blessed.

Love and Light,

La Espiritista

About the Author

La Espiritista (They/Them/Theirs pronouns) is an author, performance artist, and healer based out of Seattle, WA (occupied Duwamish land). They are a co-founder of "Share the Spirit," a small healing arts business that helps individuals clear limiting beliefs, heal energetic wounds, and open creative channels. Their art is a manifestation of their exploration of queer spirituality and sexuality.

They were born and raised in New Jersey with a mixed Peruvian and Cuban heritage. From a young age they had a deep connection to spirit, but also embraced their queerness and gender fluidity. There wasn't space for them to express their holistic self due to the constraints of most organized faiths. Their experience of religious trauma has led them to a path of healing and integration of the whole being.

La Espiritista has performed their poetry nationally and internationally in venues such as Seattle Poetry Slam, Nuyorican Poets Café, Highline College, Vancouver B.C. Red Gate's Art Society, UC Davis, and more.

About the Illustrator

Nur Shojai is a painter, illustrator, and facilitator based in Vancouver, Canada. Her favorite mediums are oil and watercolor and her work explores spiritual journey and metaphors in nature.

She grew up witnessing many ways of life; being of Persian descent and living in Canada, United States, Colombia, and Bolivia. Her formative years spent in Latin America infused her spirit with passion, color, and rhythm. From a young age her three loves were art, animals, and dance.

Nur studied environmental science and international relations at the University of British Columbia. For over a decade she has been dedicated to programs empowering children and youth with a vision of social transformation. She began pursuing a career in the arts in 2014 and completed an Artist Residency with ArtQuake Society in Vancouver. She has created curriculum and facilitated mural projects and art workshops for youth. She apprenticed and studied under award-winning professional artists in London, UK, and Seattle, WA.

www.nurshojai.com
@nurshojaiart

Free on my Website at

www.laespiritista.com

Visit my website and receive healing in various of ways:

- Join email list and receive self-love affirmations "25 Things I Have Learned" in PDF form.

- Read weekly blog excerpts based off the spiritual process of this book: "Release, Renewal, Retreat, and Rebirth."

- Read weekly meditations and in-depth guidance for your personal journey.

- Listen to free samples of performance pieces on topics such as healing, self-love, spirituality, clearing energetic blocks, soulful wisdom, embracing gender and sexuality, and more.

- Watch free 3-5 min motivational talks about holistic healing.

- Subscribe to email list and receive monthly eNewsletter containing up to date information from La Espiritista, free audio and video on spiritual wisdom, exclusive promotions, and more. Stay connected!

- Receive notice of when upcoming books will be released.

Find me on Instagram

@laespiritista

Made in the USA
Columbia, SC
17 July 2019